FRACTALS
&
MNEMONICS

WARNING

Do **not** look
Do **not** ask
Do **not** listen

Do **not** worry
Do **not** speak
Do **not** question

Do **not** turn
Do **not** think
Do **not** refuse

Do **not** do
Do **not**hing
Do **not** do this

FRACTALS & MNEMONICS

JAMIE INGLIS

© PROHIBITED PUBLICATIONS
MMVIII

fractals & mnemonics
© Jamie Inglis 1996. All rights reserved.
Second Edition 2008
ISBN 978-0-9556810-0-4

The right of Jamie Inglis to be identified as the author of this work has been asserted by him in accordance with the Copyright, Designs and Patents Act, 1998.

Contact the author
info@jamieinglis.com

Many thanks to **Alex Nisbet** for kind permission to reproduce a fractal from **'Karaoke Kabuki'** one of *The Actor Series* on the cover; and the full image in b&w on p77.
www.alexnisbet.com

Burning the Page - Internet Services
www.burningthepage.com

The Poetry Index
www.poetry-index.com

The Disorganised Society
www.disorganised.org

Printed by Lulu
www.lulu.com/content/1200507

Published by
PROHIBITED PUBLICATIONS
79 Bruntsfield Place
Edinburgh
EH10 4HG
Scotland
www.prohibitedpublications.com

By the same author

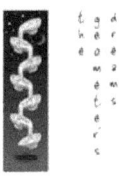

the geometer's dreams

fractals & mnemonics

hold on

gluon notes

FRACTALS & MNEMONICS

previously

The Geometer and the Chinese Box	1
First contact, train to Edinburgh	2
Hope in our time	3
Meeting a doubt ?	4
Days of looking backwards and forwards	6

from France

Flamingo Fire	9
Waiting in Soulliac	10
Early light in Saint-Remy	11
Cyrano in Bergerac	12
Choosing a Tattoo on the Train to Bergerac	13
Bordeaux Gare	14

from Albania

For Mijellin	19
Martyrs of 39	20
Early evening coffee at the Palace of Culture	21
Durres Promenade	22
Nature whispers the loudest song	23
Tirana Medicine	24
Different Eyes	25
Small states again	26

from a frontline living room

Another Saddam war	31
Medical call up November 1990	32
Unloading at Prestwick	33
Gulf War One plus one	34
Final letter	35

from Cyberville

Mockquake	39
New Words For Today	40
Ode to Postscript Printers	41
Burgerland	42
Pinball Graveyard	43
The New Alchemists	44

eventually

Earth's time of darkness comes again	47
Hearts of Darkness	49
The end of The Lakes	50
Empty Cardboard Box	51
Formal	53
Bold yet Fluid	55
Balance	57

from new neologisms

infoblur	61
gigadust	63
timetaps	65
chaodays	67
logoblur	69
timeexit	71

colophon

some friends	75

previously

	CHINESE	**AND**	**THE**
	BOX	**THE**	**GEOMETER**
prying	from	for	Looking
eyes.	all,	secrets.	at
	but	Hidden	life

First contact, train to Edinburgh

The fragile nectar of first contact
with hastily averted eyes
or inadvertent touch.

An exploration of potential meaning
in that moment of meeting
of two strangers, unknown till now.

But now that moment has altered
and lack of strangeness

beckons.
An intermingling of lines
perhaps love, perhaps passion
perhaps hate, perhaps danger.

Continuation as an instant decision
in a moment
of subliminal processes
hidden from interception by a conscious
Touch.

Hope in our time

The Hope syndrome
Genetic part of every psyche

The Hope complex
A belief made purpose

The Hope phenomenon
The credo of our time

The Hope cartel
Sold to us a panacea

The Hope agenda
For only a limited few

The Hope debate
Our future lowered to discussion

The Hope dilemma
The choices of Solomon

The Hope gallery
An exhibition of dreams

The Hope market
The province of aspirations

Meeting a doubt ?

On my way to Tuvalu
I met an enquiring man.
He asked about you,
said he was you're biggest fan.

Its a long trip there,
so we had naturally got to talking.
He had a certain vocal flare,
a natural talent for storytelling.

We chatted about mutual friends,
both of us had known.
A means to ends,
as all other company had flown.

That was when he asked,
that slipped in question.
All about you subtly masked,
as simple friendship, without pretension.

My first reply was genial, bland,
'doing well', and making a joke.
Not intending sleight of hand,
he seemed to be a decent bloke.

And similarly on we went,
a pleasing way to pass a journey.
Each pursuing our natural bent,
to conversation as opening play.

Then came the second thrust,
with a marked, more probing feel.
And a sense of danger felt,
of unease, a shiver of steel.

Naturally, my reply gently parried,
curious of his knowledge and intent.
But in response, he only dallied,
making light, with an easy jest.

And similarly on we went,
a pleasing way to pass a journey.
Each pursuing our natural bent,
for conversation as closing play.

We arrived at Tuvalu,
parting without leaving a clue.
What secret did he know of you,
leaving a taste of something blue;
hinting of something only he knew.

Days of looking backwards and forwards

Just seem to follow us around
as a slowly accumulating set
packing them up from a long way out
marked 'wanted on voyage'.

Every chance encounter leads us here.
To think it is to make it so.

from France

FLAMINGO FIRE

At darkening time
on Lyon landscape
the flamingos fire
the fading sky.

Wheels of flame
spiral high overhead
riding the thermals
rising from the Camargue.

WAITING IN SOULLIAC

One hundred tables
laid every day.
One hundred tablecloths,
covers, cutlery, glasses, plates, dressing,
correct each way.
Two hundred settings,
laid for those who will pay.

One hundred tables,
cleared every day.
Two hundred dishes,
for tourists who didn't stay.
One weary waiter,
at the end of every day.

EARLY LIGHT IN SAINT-REMY

Heats the mornings air for boules
beyond the clean wood
where metal jars the silent air.
Single sharp pastis starting
springs first mistless day.

Unchilling the pavement seats.
Where sharp short blacks
awake afresh the sense
of living here, Saint-Remy, today.

Cyrano in Bergerac

A poet fresh, from a play
set in concrete, here to stay.

Just a bit, of a liberty
considering he never
passed this way.

CHOOSING A TATTOO ON THE TRAIN TO BERGERAC

What best suits you
from the catalogue in view.
As the train rattles through,
which one to pursue.

The strangers are gaping
as they see you in the making.
A multitude of signals,
yours for the taking.

Something small and simple
to hide that hated pimple,
or complement that dimple.
Perhaps a rose, on a pink nipple.

A Gothic patch to cover your back
but don't want to look like a motorcycle hack.
You're name, of course, for when I get back.
Where to place, that's the right track.

BORDEAUX GARE

Above Bordeaux gare
a single drapeau gently flaps
as darkness lightly drops.
And balls of light flicker bright
an orange glow of spheres alight
illuminate the station bright.

Buses halt, disgorge, depart.
Traffic becomes taxis then goes.
Information signs flickering without ceasing.
Late cafes catch the last stragglers.
The jazz notes drift on the square.
A bright gare clock strikes the end of day.

from Albania

For Mijellin

When I listen, all I hear
are the songs of the heart, of poverty and sadness.
And when I look, all I see
are signs of the mind, painful to see.

What do I know of this world here
so distant from mine.
My life feels so out of time
that I must retreat to my dream.

Why, when I ask, is this so strange
the answers come tumbling but senseless.
For here this is real, if only tonight,
and tomorrow, we shall all wake to this.

Martyrs of 39

The memorial to the martyrs of 39
has faded now, and the glass is all gone.
Pillboxes fill the tranquil gardens,
where old men sit, playing chess
and reminiscing of these bright days.
Before the photos were removed,
and the martyrs became faceless.
Now their glory and their grace is gone,
the garden to weeds and war preparations.
Their fight is a long time over,
and the next already begun.
These brave martyrs, soon dust and gone.

EARLY EVENING COFFEE AT THE PALACE OF CULTURE

The heart of Skandeberg
sings in the darkness.
A thousand voices ache
in poverty and sadness.

After the heat of the day
every space is part of the crowd.
Making a little, little business,
not a single head is bowed.

Islam wails from the new minaret
opposite communist murals, proclaiming Albania.
The old ideas are hard to forget
as market fever grips Tirana.

In the heart of Skandeberg
the deals are constantly done.
But poverty and sadness, are constant things,
no future will be harder won.

DURRES PROMENADE

When I miss you most
is when the sun is sinking into the sea.
And the last rays cast a chill glare
along the seafront of people walking.
Mostly they are couples courting or together.
Sometimes with young babies
or sometimes with children in Sunday best.
Then there are the girls, also dressed
holding hands, in two's and three's.
And the young men their macho best
all walking in the twilight promenade.
And I sit as they pass and stare.
This is when I miss you most.

NATURE WHISPERS THE LOUDEST SONG

Drinking raki in the rain
under a flickering Durres lighthouse beam.
While the storm rages up the Adriatic
sheets of lightning curtain the horizon.
Thunder rocks the ice in the glass
as the coffee chills in the raindrop deluge.

Then, as the storm moves on past,
and while the glow from the raki still lasts;
a dazzling flash horizon long;
and thunder booming, on and on;
reminding us,
nature whispers the loudest song.

TIRANA MEDICINE

He showed me his container.
It was for the ulcer drug,
Ranitidine.
And it was empty.

I recognised the drug.
Very expensive,
my boss is on it,
(he's under a lot of stress you know),
swears by it.
Can go out, have a few drinks,
feel fine.
Not in Tirana,
with his empty container.

DIFFERENT EYES

So many landings
in different times
in different places.

So many landings
as different people
among different friends.

So many landings
from different lives
for different reasons.

So many landings
to different views
and different eyes.

SMALL STATES AGAIN

Returning to the time of small states.
When there was Thrace
at war with Macedonia.
And the world was tribes again
disputing over ground,
that was rightfully theirs,
since the time of there forebears.
And the small state comes again.
Our civilisation is ending,
as so many others have before this,
by descending into anarchy.
Small states again.

from a frontline living room

of the Gulf War

Another Saddam war

Once more we stand on the brink
of war in a hot, distant land.
Where the economics of oil drag us
to protect these black desert fields.
Where a million men fresh from trenches
defend the will of a new Saladin.
Who defiles the new found child of peace
with his dreams of empire and glory.
In a world readjusting to friendship
where nations return armies home quietly,
the soldiers no longer required now.
Yet one is still driven to soldier
and we must make ready, for war in Islam.

Medical call up November 1990

The preparations for war go on as before,
a wearisome task, even viewed from afar.
Propaganda, powerful, persistent, persuasive.

The preparations for war come closer to home,
more medics are called, as killing needs care.
Personal, conscripted to care.

The preparations for war affect us all,
sleepwalking to war, blindfolded to peace.
Passing rotation limits, talked out negotiations.

The preparations for war unstoppable now,
defeating crisis fatigue in fragile alliance.
Resolutions, reinforcements, recruitment, resolve

The preparations for war unavoidable now,
Christmas parcels sent, the war comes after.
C^3I in place, counting in days, dates and deadlines.

The preparations for war almost complete,
carols fill the Eastern desert, washing faces in winters fear.
PONTI's ordered to the rear.

The preparations for war divide us all.

Unloading at Prestwick

I see a coffin on TV today.
A homecoming coffin,
a local coffin, coming home.
Crying at death,
no longer faceless.
Now a face,
removed by fire of war.
Only the rictus remains,
and the lack of understanding.

Gulf War One plus one

One year passes from the start of war
hidden it continues obscured from view.
Many peoples forgotten after the storm
destroyed our homes, poisoned our land.

Alone in the mountains far from shelter
the touch of cold, twist of hunger.
Slowing each body, starving each mind
destroying our lives, driven from our land.

Alone in the desert far from shelter
poisoned black oases and darkness descending.
Expelled waste, herded and evicted
destroyed our people, lamenting our land.

Final letter

After he came home, sealed from view,
a day had passed, perhaps two.
When pain came
unbidden again.

A letter from the shadows
before death, out of time flows.
A final, final parting word
no way to send back a reply.

from Cyberville

MOCKQUAKE

Every year
when they practice
the Mockquake in Tokyo
it rocks the world.

The six wise men
of seismological science
announce abnormal data.
So take to the land.

The pulse to the city
starts out to sea
and takes nine seconds
to reach the superstructures.

Where tremors fracture
gas, glass and bodies.
Silence from Tokyo
shakes the world.

NEW WORDS FOR TODAY

Confidential

In Confidence

Draft in Confidence

In Strict Confidence

Commercial in Confidence

Restricted Access

Most Secret

Password protected

Patent Pending

Virus Checking

Unauthorised Possession is Illegal

Secret Society

Publication Prohibited

ODE TO POSTSCRIPT PRINTERS

We thought we were clever
when we invented computers.
But they got viruses too.
New ones every day,
infected like us.
And passing it on
and on, and on, *and on,*
ανδ ον, ☊■ ♎🗐 □■ ☊■♎ □■,

Error Message :   Programme has crashed
Error Message :   Programme has crashed
Error Message :   Programme has crashed

C:\>System access failure #13

General Protection Fault0M075P038

Switch off and call your helpline

BURGERLAND

Back in Burgerland
where no-one cares
what they eat or shit.

McDonalds promise to brighten up our lives
as the forests vanish
warming the planet degree by degree.
Then it seams our lives will brighten
as the sun heats our sky.

Back in Burgerland,
cardboard in,
cardboard and greenhouse gasses out.
Convenience is King.

Pinball Graveyard

Where do all the old machines go?
When the electromagnets weaken,
the flippers begin to stick,
and the silver ball looses its shine.

Where do all the old machines go?
When the lights fail to flash,
the bumpers fail to bounce,
and the tilt is no longer a tremble.

Where do all the old machines go?
When the specials always light,
the excitement begins to fade,
and everyone scores the replay.

THE NEW ALCHEMISTS

Smart machines modelling nature
Smart structures from the
New alchemists
Smart models

Smart molecules
Smart materials

Smart textiles
Smart piezo-electrics
Smart satellites
Smart buildings

Smart new alchemist

Soft ? brains

eventually

EARTH'S TIME OF DARKNESS COMES AGAIN

Late start,
to the fluorocarbon debate.
The herald of oblivion,
to the time of darkness again.

Depletion of the ozone layer,
means hide from the sun.
Three thousand years ago
Bronze age Scotland
changed forever.
This change forever comes again.

It was once a very different world
when a generation of Scots
will once again abandon their land,
leaving the wasteland,
far to the north.

The dusting of Hecla III
went unnoticed in 1150,

but the trees stopped growing.
Volcanoes, acid, poor climate,
slows the trees.
Marasmus, Rabal, Etna, Santorini, Krakatoa, Tambora.

The time of darkness,
comes again.
Benjamin Franklin's first conjecture,
leads to Tambora,
and the year without a summer, 1816.
During the obscuration of the sun,
Byron speaks Darkness.

The aerosols spread round the stratosphere,
scattering the sunlight,
chilling the oceans.
Winters chilling.

The ozone deviation has appeared.
Chloroflurocarbons sensitised the trigger
for the next big volcano to erupt.

HEARTS OF DARKNESS

Hearts of darkness
pacing empty city streets.

Isolated and alone, fleeing
the fray of life in the city,
whose heart has gone.
Bled away, by greed and fear,
by hearts so blue.

How could they do this thing
to hearts that were young.
Before they became
hearts of darkness.

THE END OF THE LAKES

The lakes are shrinking and dying
    shrivelling, as new land appears around their rims.

The lakes are poisoned, gasping and dying,
    polluted waters soak the land.

Lake Baikal, the great lake is dying,
    the steppes spreading, shrinking the shore.

Lake Chad, the desert lake is dying,
    the Sahara spreading further south.

The largest lakes are dying first,
    as the earth begins, a nightmare thirst.

EMPTY CARDBOARD BOX

I do not waste my dreams on sleep
I dream my dreams by day.

Living these dreams
I am just unable to lock away.

I do not dream of islands
but follow the flow by day.

Living these dreams
in the harsh light of play.

I do not dream of flying
nothing clouds my dreams by day.

Living this dream
of finding somewhere to stay.

FORMAL

BOLD YET FLUID

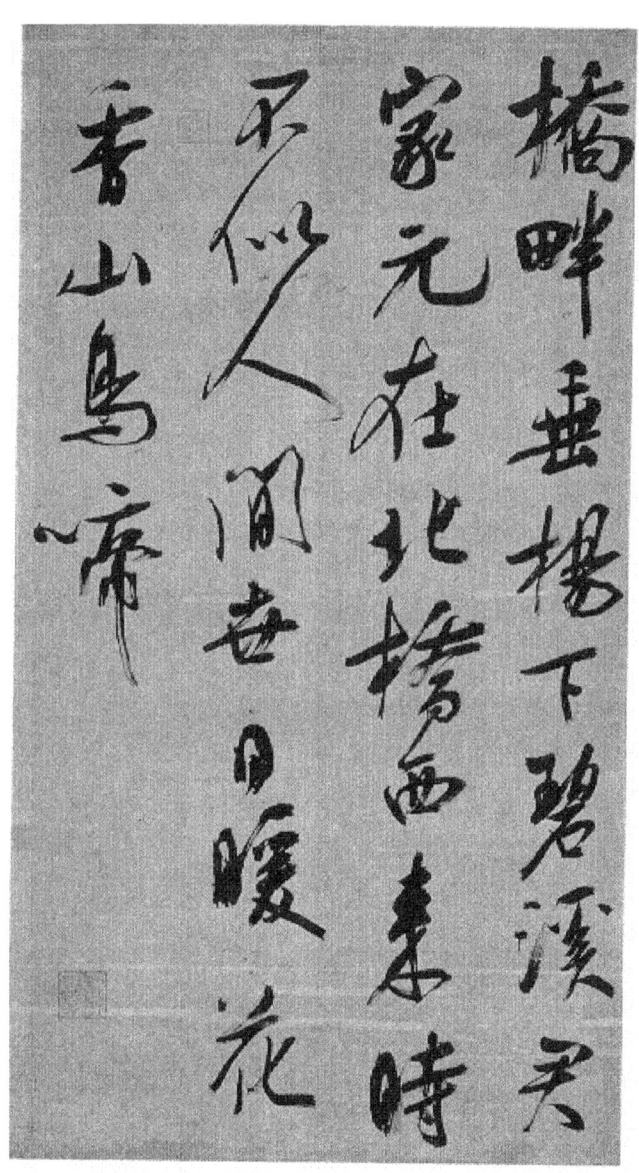

BALANCE

from new neologisms

INFOBLUR

Adrift amid oceans of expanding information,
at our fingertips and before our eyes.

Six billion data trails and all human knowledge,
at our fingertips and before our eyes.

www.infoblur.com

GIGADUST

A supervolcano shakes the planet's plates,
the ejecta slowly darkens the sun.

Massive dust clouds merge around the planet,
gigadust forms and leads to winter.

www.gigadust.com

TIMETAPS

Shocks from the cracks in history,
events outwith the human record.

Outliers from the land of the past,
change outwith the human record.

www.timetaps.com

CHAODAYS

Emerging strings of chaotic events,
merge and menace normal time.

Butterfly signs each and every day,
buffet and bruise normal time.

www.chaodays.com

LOGOBLUR

Corporate icons fade to grey.
Corporate mantras forgotten today.

Corporate religions lose their way.
Corporate empire has had its day.

www.logoblur.com

TIMEEXIT

Step outside the constant flow,
freeze each moment before the next.

An Einstein bridge outside time,
living each moment before the next.

www.timeexit.com

colophon

Some friends
from afar
visit today
and somehow
seem, to stay,
even after
they, have gone.

Karaoke Kabuki by Alex Nisbet

next

hold on

jamie inglis

ISBN 978-0-9556810-0-4

© PROHIBITED PUBLICATIONS

MMVIII

www.prohibitedpublications.com